D0753668

MMA GREATS

WITH THE RAVEN

BY LORI POLYDOROS

Reading Consultant:
Barbara J. Fox
Professor Emerita
North Carolina State University

CAPSTONE PRESS
a capstone imprint

Blazers is published by Capstone Press,
1710 Roe Crest Drive, North Mankato, Minnesota, 56003
www.capstonepub.com

Library of Congress Cataloging-in-Publication Data
Polydoros, Lori, 1968–
    MMA greats / by Lori Polydoros.
    p. cm.—(Blazers. Best of the best.)
    Includes bibliographical references and index.
    Summary: "Lists and describe the best fighters in mixed martial arts, from the past
and present"—Provided by publisher.
ISBN 978-1-4296-8433-0 (library binding)
ISBN 978-1-62065-205-3 (ebook PDF)
1. Mixed martial arts—Juvenile literature. I. Title.
GV1102.7.M59P67 2013
796.815—dc23   2012000114

Editorial Credits
Mandy Robbins, editor; Kyle Grenz, designer; Laura Manthe, production specialist

Photo Credits
Getty Images: Jon Kopaloff, 17, 23, Zuffa LLC, 7, Zuffa LLC/Al Bello, 28-29, Zuffa LLC/Donald
Miralle, 20-21, Zuffa LLC/Josh Hedges, cover (bottom), 10-11, 12-13, 18-19; Newscom: Cal
Sport Media/John Green, 26-27, CSM/Cal Sport Media/Josh Thompson, 14-15, Getty Images/
AFP/Rogerio Barbosa, 1 (top), Icon SMI, cover (top), 1 (bottom), 8-9, MOA WENN Photos/
Mary Ann Owen, 4-5, UPI/Roger Williams, 24

Artistic Effects
Shutterstock: nobeastsofierce

Printed in the United States of America in Stevens Point, Wisconsin.
032012   006678WZF12

TABLE OF CONTENTS

IN THE OCTAGON

MMA WEIGHT CLASSES

Weight Class	Weight in Pounds
Bantamweight	126-135
Featherweight	136-145
Lightweight	146-155
Welterweight	156-170
Middleweight	171-185
Light Heavyweight	186-205
Heavyweight	206-265

Mixed martial arts (MMA) competitors face off in an eight-sided ring. They fight with wrestling and **martial arts** moves. The match lasts until someone gives in or can't fight anymore. Check out the greats of this exciting sport.

mixed martial arts–a full-combat sport that combines wrestling moves with martial arts moves

martial arts–styles of self-defense and fighting; tae kwon do, judo, and karate are examples of martial arts

DAN SEVERN

(1958-)

Dan Severn is the **knockout** king. He earned his 99th win at age 53. Dan joined the **Ultimate Fighting Championship** (UFC) Hall of Fame in 2005.

knockout–a victory in which a fighter's opponent is unable to get up after being knocked to the ground

Ultimate Fighting Championship–an American mixed martial arts promotion company that hosts the top-ranked fighters and events around the world

FACT Dan held the UFC Heavyweight Championship and a professional wrestling title at the same time. No other fighter has done this.

GEORGES ST-PIERRE

(1981-)

Georges St-Pierre is one of the best UFC fighters. As a kid, he learned karate to defend himself against a school bully. Today Georges boxes, wrestles, and does Brazilian **jujitsu**.

jujitsu–a form of martial arts that focuses on ground fighting

MATT HUGHES

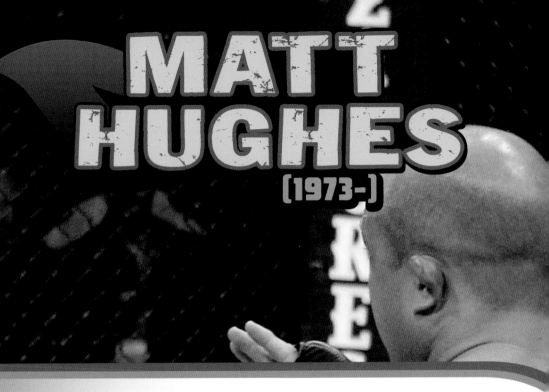

MATT HUGHES
(1973-)

Matt Hughes joined the UFC Hall of Fame in 2010. He holds the record for winning the most UFC fights. Matt has defended the championship belt seven times.

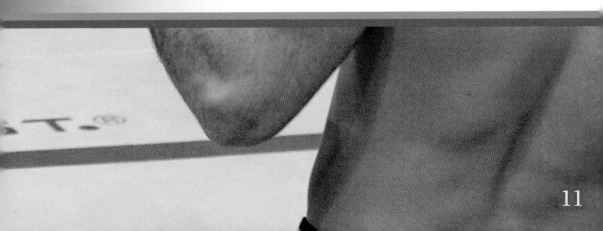

ANDERSON SILVA

FACT Anderson has black belts in tae kwon do, judo, and Brazilian jujitsu.

ANDERSON SILVA

(1975-)

Anderson Silva uses his **Muay Thai** skills to make quick strikes. By 2012, he had won 15 UFC fights in a row. That's the longest winning streak in UFC history.

Muay Thai–a combat sport from Thailand that uses stand-up striking

CHUCK LIDDELL

CHUCK LIDDELL
(1969-)

Chuck Liddell was one of the first UFC fighters to use karate and kickboxing moves. Chuck's bold style brought many fans to the sport.

FACT Chuck won the Light Heavyweight Championship in 2004. He held it for three years before losing it to Quinton Jackson.

MARK COLEMAN

(1964-)

Mark Coleman is a U.S. Olympic wrestler and a mixed martial artist. He used his wrestling background to create a fighting style called "ground and pound." Mark takes his opponent to the ground and strikes him.

FACT Mark's nickname is "The Godfather of Ground and Pound."

MARK COLEMAN

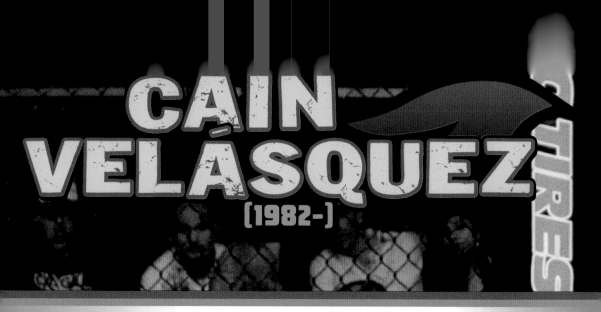

CAIN VELÁSQUEZ
(1982-)

Former UFC Heavyweight
Champion Cain Velásquez went
undefeated for nine matches.
In his first fight, he knocked out
his opponent in the first **round**.

undefeated–unbeaten; a fighter who
has won every match

round–a period of play in a sport or contest; regular MMA
fights have three rounds and title fights have five rounds

CAIN VELÁSQUEZ

FACT Cain lost the Heavyweight title to Junior dos Santos in 2011. It was his first-ever loss.

TITO ORTIZ

TITO ORTIZ

(1975-)

Tito Ortiz started fighting in the UFC while he was in college. He held the UFC Light Heavyweight title for three years. Only Anderson Silva has held it longer.

FRANK SHAMROCK

(1972-)

Frank Shamrock was the first UFC Middleweight Champion. Frank left the UFC as a five-time, undefeated champion. Frank beat one fighter in 14 seconds and another in 20!

FACT Frank had a 10-year winning streak. During that time he won 12 fights.

KEN SHAMROCK

(1964-)

Ken Shamrock is Frank's brother and another early UFC fighter. He defeated Dan Severn to become the first UFC Superfight Heavyweight Champion.

ROYCE GRACIE

(1966-)

Royce Gracie helped create the UFC. He often beat opponents bigger than himself. In 1993 Royce became the first UFC Champion.

ROYCE GRACIE

FACT Royce is the only fighter to beat four opponents in one night.

FACT Randy is the oldest UFC title holder. He won his last Heavyweight Championship at age 44.

RANDY COUTURE
(1963-)

Randy Couture was the first fighter to win two different weight class titles. He is a three-time UFC Heavyweight Champion. Randy also won the Lightweight Championship twice.

GLOSSARY

jujitsu (jih-JOOT-soo)—a martial art that focuses on ground fighting

knockout (NOK-out)—a victory in which a fighter's opponent is unable to get up after being knocked to the ground

martial arts (MAR-shuhl ARTS)—styles of self-defense and fighting; tae kwon do, judo, and karate are examples of martial arts

mixed martial arts (MIXT MAR-shuhl ARTS)—a full-combat sport combining wrestling and martial arts moves

Muay Thai (MY TIE)—a combat sport from Thailand that uses stand-up striking

round (ROUND)—a period of play in a sport or contest

Ultimate Fighting Championship (UHL-tuh-mit FITE-ing CHAM-pee-uhn-ship)—an American mixed martial arts promotion company that hosts the top-ranked fighters and events around the world

undefeated (un-dih-FEET-id)—unbeaten

READ MORE

Hamilton, John. *Greatest Hits.* Xtreme UFC. Edina, Minn.: ABDO Pub. Co., 2011.

O'Shei, Tim. *Muay Thai.* Martial Arts. Mankato, Minn.: Capstone Press, 2009.

Wiseman, Blaine. *Ultimate Fighting: Sporting. Championships.* New York: Weigl Publishers, 2011.

INTERNET SITES

FactHound offers a safe, fun way to find Internet sites related to this book. All of the sites on FactHound have been researched by our staff.

Here's all you do:

Visit *www.facthound.com*

Type in this code: 9781429684330

INDEX